The Art of Falling
In Love Again

Also by Franny Arrieta

We're Meant to Be / We're Not Meant to Be

The Art of Falling In Love Again

FRANNY ARRIETA

Andrews McMeel
PUBLISHING®

Andrews McMeel Publishing
a division of Andrews McMeel Universal
1130 Walnut Street, Kansas City, Missouri 64106

www.andrewsmcmeel.com

24 25 26 27 28 TEN 10 9 8 7 6 5 4 3 2 1

ISBN: 978-1-5248-9542-6

Library of Congress Control Number: 2024941027

Editor: Patty Rice
Art Director: Tiffany Meairs
Production Editor: Jasmine Lim
Production Manager: Beth Steiner

ATTENTION: SCHOOLS AND BUSINESSES
Andrews McMeel books are available at quantity discounts with bulk purchase for educational, business, or sales promotional use. For information, please e-mail the Andrews McMeel Publishing Special Sales Department: sales@andrewsmcmeel.com.

Dedicated to my forever love

I've deleted and typed these words many times.
I hope whoever reads this knows that love exists.
It always has, and it always will.
Whether you've never been in love, scared to fall in love,
or trying to fall in love again.
This book is for you.
Don't be scared to feel the most beautiful thing this world has to
offer us.
I pushed it away far too many times and all that did was lead
me into darkness.
I know it's scary.
But regardless of any fear, please remember to love yourself.
Take care of your heart.
Walk away if you need to walk away.
Run toward it if it will heal you.
You come first.
Always remember, the art of falling in love starts with you.

THE FINE LINE OF LOVE AND HATING MYSELF

A promise is never broken
I promise I'll continue holding
On to the words that I've said
I'll try my best till the very end

But if the end comes soon
And our time is up
Sorry for my compromised heart
It's all on a fine line cusp

I CAN'T BE LOVED RIGHT NOW

I'm sorry I'm difficult to love right now
My heart still hurts

Not because of him
But only because of me

Many say, "It's ok, it'll get easier"
But I'm sorry I agree to disagree

ALL I FEAR IS WHO'S IN THE MIRROR

Who is that?
Can't be me?
I don't recognize her?
Why can't I recognize her?

I'm scared
Can someone help me?
But I don't want help
Why don't I want help?

She fears to touch

Being alone is beautiful

She can't give much

I'm standing at my own funeral

I DON'T KNOW WHAT TO SAY WHEN PEOPLE ASK ABOUT YOU

I don't really know . . .

(I've almost said *baby*
But you're not mine

I've almost said *I love you*
But I'm not in love with you

We kiss goodbye
But never in front of others

We talk every day
But we don't have to)

. . . what this is

IN YOUR ARMS LIKE YOU DO EVERY NIGHT, ABOVE YOUR SHOULDER AND RIGHT UNDER YOUR CHIN

"Just like that?"

"Yes, just like that."

LONER

Oh how beautiful
To love the loneliness
I once feared
And oh how beautiful
It is to finally hear
The conversations in my head
And oh how beautiful
The world can look
Without constant noise
And oh how beautiful
To finally see beauty
In the loneliness
I once feared

HENRY

AKA "PAPAS"

I PROMISE THIS WAR WILL END SOON (I HOPE)

Trust me when I say
I've been fighting
For a place
For you in my heart

Not a war I would
Have ever asked for
Or would
Ever bear to start

But you never started the war
You came when it was ending

I didn't think it was possible
While my heart was mending

But you came
And you're here now

So I'm sorry
For all the loud

But I promise I'll keep fighting

I won't give up like it's nothing

COLDHEARTED IS AN UNDERSTATEMENT

I used to be warm
A feeling I miss

I used to love anything
My favorite good morning kiss

But now my new lovers
Tell me they're scared

Scared they'll never hear my heart
Or feel the touch of it bare

Behind this wall
I live in what I've built

Trying to keep warm
Trying to hide from the guilt

With my soul and my heart
Forever it stays frozen

All I have left is me, God, some prayer
And a little bit of devotion

GOOD MORNING

YOU'RE THE ONLY REASON I WAKE UP
I NEVER WANT TO WAKE UP
MY DREAMS HAVE BEEN LOVELY
MY DREAMS TEND TO SAVE ME

6:57 AM

(COULDN'T SLEEP
LAST NIGHT)

"LOVE YOU" NOT "I LOVE YOU"

We love each other
We've seen each other naked
We hold each other tight
Until the other has awakened

To,
Me
I love You
More and more
Every single day
You are my
favorite thing
to come home
From,
You

I KNOW GOD UNDERSTANDS ME

God

Please

I am pleading

You detach me

From feeling everything

And nothing

All at the same time

"where's the finish line?"

- growth
- losing friends
- where am I meant to be!

I don't think
a finish line
exists...

DO
YOU?

I FEEL BROKEN

I see my future so clearly . . .

Happiness in my eyes
A beautiful home
My children laughing
But where is the stone

ANXIETY HAS GOTTEN A LITTLE LOUDER

My skin is falling
My bones are showing
My eyes are closing
????

It just keeps going.

LET'S SAY WE'RE NOT SCARED

We've always feared falling
But we've fallen already

What do we do?
We keep the heart steady

But as fear continues
To be our best friend

We hide our dark thoughts
And keep playing pretend

PLEASE TEACH ME

I don't know if I'm ready for your love . . .

A love you would call kind
So delicately sweet and light

Sweet like our morning coffee

My eyes weep
My heart breaks
My hands shake
Knowing my love isn't as sweet

It used to be sweet . . .

Sweeter than our morning coffee
But my hands are shaking too hard

And unfortunately I've spilt it all

ME + HENRY

4/6/24

SHOT BY CALEB

HEAVY TOWEL

I almost threw in the towel tonight
It's just gotten so heavy

Heavy from our talks
The thoughts are too many

My trauma is yelling
Oh how nice it's the cherry

I'm thinking of you
It's some baggage to carry

STARGAZING

Walking home

You stop me quick

Looking into my eyes

To give me one last kiss

It's too soon to say *I love you*

So we stare a little longer

And that's how we say *I love you*

Who knew our eyes spoke stronger

THERAPY

After a year of only having half
a heart,
I finally felt whole again.
I was smiling
and laughing. My tears had
finally dried up.
But then I met you. And everything
I thought healed
came right back to the surface.
Everything that I never
knew existed, existed more than
anything in my life.
All because I
opened my heart again.
All because
I let my heart love again.
I want to
say *thank you*, but all
I really want
to say is
I'm sorry.

AND THIS IS ALL A PART OF OUR STORY NOW

Every scream

Every "I can't make it"

Every flower I picked

Every "No you'll kill it"

Every cry for help

Every "I can't fake it"

Every chapter that's closed

Every "I'm happy it's finished"

I WISH YOU WERE HERE

7/15/23

OUCH

My heart has ached
For a love like yours
But it aches even more
Now that I have it

I asked for roses
On my twenty-sixth birthday
And when I got them
They pinched my stomach

our perfect day

my perfect day

FRIENDS

If you look too hard
You'll never find it

If you don't look at all
God will place it in your hands

Love can be so blind
But never blind enough

It will one day find you
Please just trust

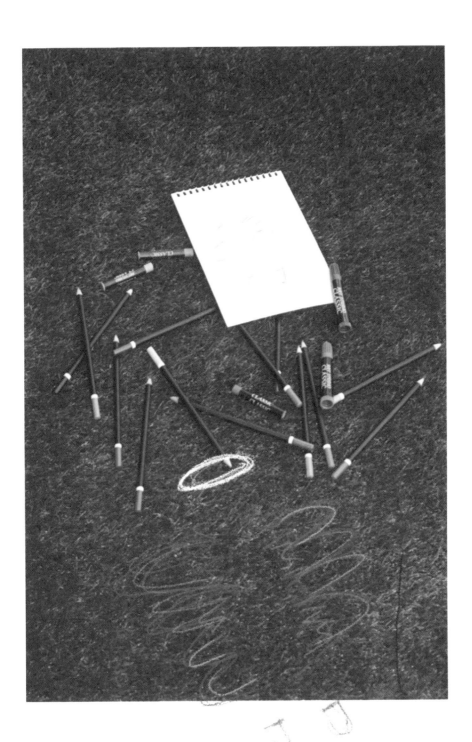

SOMETIMES YOU JUST WAKE UP FOR A COUPLE DRINKS

The morning is young
    Wake up
I'm in my head
    Deep breaths
        The night came quick
            One blink
        The night is young
            Two drinks

SANTA BARBARA AGAIN

I made it back to Santa Barbara with someone
new. I can't really say which trip was better,
but I can say they were both different. The old
trip was beautifully sad, while the new trip was
perfectly planned. I just pray that the new trip
doesn't turn into a beautifully sad one too. If
it does, I don't think I'd ever go back; I'd have
to find somewhere new.

TRAUMA HAS ME WORRIED

My pillow is flooded
I cry at night thinking
If we don't ever make it
I will lose you forever

Your heart is mine now
I could never lose you
So let us pray and say,
"God please keep us together"

But if God thinks different
Maybe we can be friends?
Whatever happens my love
It will be all for the better

I THINK MY BAGS ARE FULL

I packed every
Stuffed animal
That watched me cry

I packed the
Letters I wrote
On the 4th of July

I packed the photos
That remind me of
Every hard goodbye

I packed the world
That held me down
How could I ever fly

you won ?

(won ♡

I'M SCARED TOO

I know you see the red in my eyes
I know you don't know if my words are lies
I know it scares you to love a girl like me
I know you're worried I'm not the girl you see
I know you feel me pull forward and back
I know you know that I'm about to crack

GROWING PAINS

I wouldn't be able to

                tell my younger self

That what she thought

              would be a fairytale

Really just turns into

              a terrible nightmare

SORRY I CAN'T DECIDE

I THINK I
LIKE THIS
HOME BETTER

I DON'T WANT TO GROW UP

As every year comes
As every fear stays
I wish to be young
I'll even take yesterday

TWO FEET ARE A LOT TO HOLD

I've learned to love everyone
Except for you and me

But how could that be?

When all I've ever done for myself
Is hold my own two feet

But how could that be?

When all you've ever done
Is help set me free

Love To Infinity

Mom taught me
how to knit but I
never learned.

Mom taught me
how to love but I
never could.
I hope to love as much
as she can one day.

LET US BE SCARED TOGETHER (FUN!)

He was scared of losing me
But I was scared of losing myself

THE LITTLE THINGS

And all you can really ask
Is to find someone
You're happy to make
A cup of coffee
For every morning
For the rest of your life

And all you can really ask
Is to find someone
Who is happy to make
You a cup of coffee
Every morning
For the rest of your life

MY BIGGEST REGRET

Tonight I broke his heart
Tonight I broke my own heart

I'M IN A RUSH

I hope time isn't selfish
I hope it gives me enough to heal
I hope it gives me enough to fix myself
I hope it gives me enough to come back

DREAMER BOY

Thank you for keeping the dust off of my guitar
She's been lonely since I've put her down

We were best friends
Both three feet tall
Dreamers
Lovers

Scared?
Yes

I gave up on her
She never forgave me

But she told me the other day
She's happy you've been around

I told her,
"Me too"

I GRABBED TWO ANYWAYS

I grabbed a Fresca
You would've grabbed two
Dinner is ready
Oh how I miss you

LOVE ME FOR ME

You said my eyes were your favorite
My bare freckled face skin gave you chills

You embraced me when I wasn't embraceable
You stayed even though I couldn't watch films

I GET IT NOW BUT NOT THEN

If an ounce of what you said was true
On the night you left me in pieces
I finally understand why you did it
I understand that life is unpredictable
And I understand that sometimes
When darkness is the only thing in you
You have to find the light on your own

If not an ounce of what you said was true
Then you suck.

SPOKE TOO SOON

And as the words of betrayal left my lips . . .

I saw myself right in front of my eyes
I saw the girl who never would've given up
I saw the girl who would've fought for her love

Thank you for showing me that girl again
Thank you for never changing like this girl did

HONEY YOU'RE HOME

I know

    I felt like

        home, but I

            promise you'll

                find home

                    within yourself.

PRETTY BOY

Your eyes are a color
I couldn't quite figure out
But they were beautiful
And always looked at me

Your curly hair was my favorite
For sure not a doubt
You sometimes didn't like it
But I'd have to disagree

Your lips were far away
So you'd get low and crouch
You'd do anything for my kiss
And that was always guaranteed

ALL EYES ON YOU BABY

Someone asked me out the other tonight

And I politely declined

I said I have a lover waiting for me at home

But I had no lover at home

I was just thinking about you

FIVE DAYS OF HELL

And after five days I begged for him back

He took me back

Thank God he took me back

BLACK OUT

My episode was almost
As perfect
As the twilight zone

It was so perfectly bizarre
But I still
Don't understand it

I remember sitting in a gray room
With a
Voice I couldn't quite recognize

"Do it"
"Do it"
"Do it"

"No"
"No"
"No"

So I did it

TUSCANY BOY

A pure heart
A friend
He took us up the coast
Back to Tuscany

He played his favorite songs
The hot wind made me sleepy
I could tell he was happy to be here
I hope one day I'm happy to be here

UNE LETTRE D'AMOUR DE PARIS

Chasing for your love
Running quick before it goes
Paris is quite beautiful
Here's a rose before you go

All I ask is for time
To keep by my side
Paris is quite beautiful
Last night I started to cry

Attendez!
Wait!

Promise to love you better
Than the way I did before
I know your trust is gone
But I've always loved you more

AND I LOVE YOU

How could it be
That I've fallen
In love with you
Ten thousand miles away

I guess I just always have

My guards stood ten feet tall
And I could never show it
And I could never feel it
And I love you

I HOPE WE HAVE FOREVER

Time feels infinite with you
A love that feels old but new

Lipstick stains on our sheets
A cup of tea before bed

I love it
I hate it

Rushing for every moment
Slowing down for one last kiss

Time please don't ever end
I pray we always exist

Dear Diary,
_____ has been _____
Home has been perfect.
I can sit in your arms
forever and hope this
it never ends. I always
_____ _____ _____
_____ _____ _____
_____ _____ But I do
believe in _____ _____
believe _____ _____
I hope we have our
home for forever.

LIAR LIAR

I never thought I'd be writing
About being the bad guy

Feels like I'm half of hell
Holding back every cry

Perfect?
Who?
Me?
I wish I could be

But I've tried my best
Without turning a mess

Hurting you was hard
I never thought I would

Phone to my cheek
Yelling, "Yes I'm sure!"

Liar?
Who?
Me?
I guess I could be

But lying was all I could do
To not disappoint you

YOU'RE ALWAYS INVITED

I've become codependent
Exactly what I was afraid of

I've never been so close to someone
Who has safely secured my heart

Anxiously awaiting to be next to you again
Anxiously hoping you would want to attend

I hope I don't scare you as much as I scare me
I hope you don't start seeing all the things that I see

CAR CRASH

Our crashes weren't equal . . .

I lost my brakes
But you caught me

You fell asleep
But I let us both die

MOMS ARE ALWAYS RIGHT

Mom says I'm looking different

Mom says I need help

Mom says she knows what's wrong

Mom says she's a little worried

Mom says go to church

Mom says take a deep breath

LET ME LOSE A COUPLE MORE

I've lost him
I've lost her
I've lost me

He's happier now
She's moved on
I'm finally me

My heart has cracked many times
But the sun still keeps moving
I asked her, "Why?"
She said, "Sweetie, it's confusing."

Breathing is too hard
Can I be sad without pretending
I guess I can lose more
Look guys I'm still standing

SIX TWENTY-THREE AM

My
Favorite
Future
Habit
Is
Watching
The
Sunrise
On the 405

A LOSS ISN'T ALWAYS BAD

Heartache is pretty
Heartache is raw
Heartache is perfect
Heartache is lost

Pretty because it's beautiful
Raw because it teaches
Perfect because it's timing
Lost because it's gone

CALL ME BEAUTIFUL

I bought a pink ribbon to put in my hair today
I plucked my eyebrows this morning
I ordered a salad for dinner tonight

UNCONDITIONAL LOVE

A warm hug that never leaves

He said, "I hate you."
She said, "That's ok. I still love you."

Beautiful imperfections

A prayer for their safety

Tears when you look at them

A home-cooked meal

I hope one day everyone can experience
Unconditional love
Because I finally have

MY FAVORITE DRINK

Sunday morning
As the sun creeps in
Your lips are chapped
And the memory is dim

We smiled
We danced
We held each
Others hands

And as I looked in
Your eyes
I saw forever
In your plans

My nights out used to be drunk
Stained lips from my favorite wine
Nowadays they consist of you
Our bodies intertwined

MY INTRUSIVE THOUGHTS

Maybe it was supposed to be her
All along
Sixteen hundred miles between
Two hearts

A sad thought
To bare
A grim thought
I'm aware

If the path went left not right
If a flight was as easy as sitting tight

If the miles didn't exist I would guess
She would be all yours in a white dress

I LOVE COTTON CANDY

A sunset almost killed me today
I took a picture to make it last
Cotton candy skies turned purple
My car swerved left and I crashed

CAN ANYBODY HELP? I MIGHT SCREAM!

It's happening again
The push and pull
The waves have crashed
And I'm fighting to stand

Triggered?
Yes
Why?
I lost myself again

Loving you became easy
Just like our favorite pie
But as the world continued to spin
All I've done is lie

Not lie about loving you
Gosh I love you so much
But lie about loving me
Gosh where is my crutch?

OUR FIVE-HOUR CALLS

He called today just to say, "I love you."

I love you too baby

THANK YOU FOR HEARTBREAK

Heartbreak isn't always sad.
Heartbreak teaches you how to love yourself.
Heartbreak teaches you how to love them.

SHAMEFACED

Buried in my fears
We looked at each other
A little too quick

A ball swelling in
The middle of my throat
Soon to be sick

Too many eyes
Looking down
On shamefaced me

Everyone knows
What I've done
I had to set you free

Drink after drink
And I'm missing you
A little too much

I know I shouldn't do it
But I turned around
And gave you a nudge

IMPERFECT ME

For a while now I thought I had to fully be
healed to continue living life

Pausing everything was the only thing that
made sense

Perfect was what I strived for

But the funny thing is

I was never perfect

I learned to love while being as imperfect as
imperfect can be

And I can learn again

I DON'T WANT
THEM SET THEM ON
FIRE

SAY CHEESE

I'm tired of being triggered by love
I really am
I'm tired of telling others I'm traumatized
I really am

But no one understands

I cry hoping someone can help
I cry hoping someone can hear me

But how could they?
When I'm so good at smiling with tears in my eyes

I love you mommy.
I love you daddy.
I see so much of
me in the both of
you. a blessing? I'd
say, so Thank you
for never giving up
on me and I promise
I will never give up
on you. I cry thinking
you will be gone one
day. I cry hoping
you're proud of me
one day.

THE ART OF FALLING IN LOVE AGAIN

It's 6 pm and the sun has finally begun to set over the perfectly placed mountain outside of my living room window. I was gazing at it for quite some time with this recurring thought that someone else may think it's not as perfect as I do. People say beauty is in the eye of the beholder, but perfection is too. But my gaze soon became interrupted by his warm touch.

"What are you looking at?" he said.

"Oh, nothing. Just looking at the mountain. Isn't it pretty?" I asked.

"Yes, it's very pretty."

A little shocked that he agreed because this mountain really has nothing too special about it. It was green and brown, with a couple of small hills on it. I thought it looked nice, but I guess he did too.

We sat down on the couch and he started to draw me in a little closer to him. My heart began to race and my first initial reaction was to pull away. Not because I didn't love him, but because I was scared of allowing my heart to love someone again. He felt my pull.

"Is everything ok?" he asked.

As I stutter my words, I say I'm fine.

He knew something was wrong. He could read me like a book. My stomach rose to my throat. I couldn't even bear the thought of saying to him that his touch scares me. I selfishly was in a place of wanting my heart to myself.

He grabs me by the face and says,

"I know you're scared. I know everything in you wants to run. But I promise I will do everything in my whole heart to show you how much I love you. I will sit here forever for you. I will sit here and help you fix any problem you ever have. You are my forever. You are perfect. Your perfect smile. Your perfect heart. You are everything and anything I could ever want."

"But I'm nowhere near perfect. I'm so broken."

"Well . . . you're perfect to me," he says.

As a swell of tears takes over my face and breathing becomes close to impossible to do, I lay my head on his rapidly beating heart. I look up at him and say, "Thank you for loving me."

I laid my head back on his chest, and in that moment, I knew I was safe.

IF ONLY YOU CARED A LITTLE MORE

I know forever is
Never guaranteed
But gosh she loved
You so much

She loved you more
Than she loved herself
But I don't think you'll
Ever understand

The sun would shy
Away most days
But it was always
Found just for you

The world would fall
Heavy on her hands
But she always made
Room to hold you

I guess maybe you
Weren't meant to be
But maybe you both
Would have lasted a lifetime

PAST LIFE

August came quick
Three months have passed
My old life is present
We would never last

THE FIRST TIME YOU FALL IN LOVE AGAIN AFTER HEARTBREAK

You don't love them more.
You don't love them less.
You love them differently.

JANUARY

This winter rings colder than most
It hurt but felt a little too homey
Acclimated to my frigid fingers
The ripped skin is starting to look pretty

But as my head rests on your warm chest
And your heart's racing at its very best
To feel is impossible but I've tried to catch up
The feeling is heavy and I'll forever be stuck

<u>TO, ME</u>

I'm ready to love myself again.

Love,

Me

2023

Being me came easy. Being me felt perfect. I was scared of entering another year of hell, but God, thank you for another year of heaven. It wasn't all white room sunset views. The dark rooms were there too. I didn't hate them, but god, did they see me cry. Falling in love again was hard, but god, I'm so in love. I did more with my life in the last year than I ever did in the last twenty-five. Prayer has healed, and it always will. Pinching myself became habitual, and smiling until my face went numb was my favorite. Every person in my life has been godsent. Good or bad. Happy or sad. God, thank you. I know time is running out, and death is only promised. But I'm just happy that becoming me again came easily. It felt perfect.

MUAWH

How silly of me to believe that God doesn't exist
And
How silly of me to believe it could be fixed
with a kiss

BUT—I DON'T WANT TO GO ONE WAY

TO OUR HEAVENLY FATHER

May evil be destroyed around his name
And please remove all his underlying pain

The flowers you have grown today are so beautiful
The flowers you planted in his heart are even more

I cry to the thought of his sadness
You're the only one who sees me cry

I could never let him see me cry
Please don't waste your cries on me

Lord if I could have only one ask
And may this be my very last

If meeting him was only for a brief moment
Please Lord don't ever make him my opponent

ECHO

Vindictive . . .   Such an easy word to use

Vindictive . . .   Everybody thinks I'm vindictive

LET'S TRY OUR BEST

Frustration has killed me a couple times
But I'm still here so I guess I'm ok
It's never really black and white
So I'll try my best to explain the gray

I know I'm not the best with my words
And sometimes I fall and fall a little short
You ask me questions I don't have answers to
And I go home to rip the hair out of my head

I speak to the sky every night
It just seems to understand me
I close my eyes every night
Hoping you can understand me

PLASTIC BARBIES EVERYWHERE

I try to hide

Why do I care

I try to hide

I guess it's hell

I try to hide

Let's all be fair

I try to hide

I love you Claire

SECOND BREAKUP THOUGHT

I know every part of me deep down really
knows wholeheartedly, no doubt about it, not
even a second guess as far as the trenches of
my heart may go that we are meant to be, but
maybe not right now.

Dear Diary,

It's been 2 weeks since we last spoke. He cooks fine. I'm fine... I think? I do wonder how his nights are. Did he eat dinner? I hope so. I'm fine, but I miss him. Should I call him.

SAFE AND SOUND

I don't look like your past lover
A thought I keep to myself

Tall and thin
Fair as skin
I know I'm thin
But not as thin as her
She has a beautiful type of fair
Mine's a bit more yellow
I know you don't bring her up
Do you look at old photos?

I hope you don't miss her
A thought I keep to myself

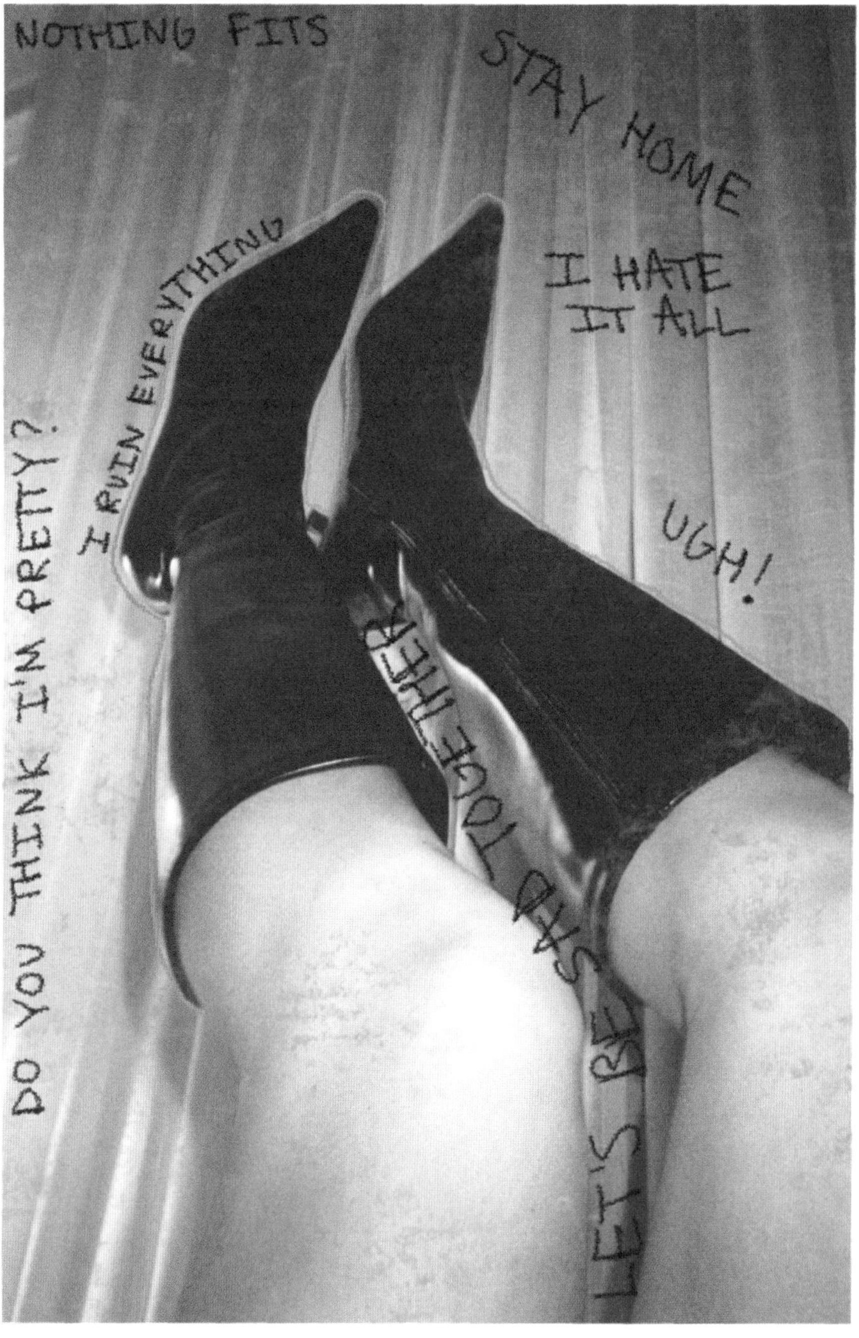
NOTHING FITS
STAY HOME
I HATE IT ALL
I RUIN EVERYTHING
DO YOU THINK I'M PRETTY?
UGH!
LET'S BE SAD TOGETHER

MY 2 PM PRAYER

God's word

God's will

God's timing

Our Father, who art in heaven, hallowed be thy name;

WE ALL NEED A FRIEND

As each year passes, the value of a low-maintenance friendship becomes very much cherished. I'm sure you've figured it out on your own, but life is already hard to survive. Checking up on yourself is difficult, and checking up on others is close to impossible. The anxiety of disappointing others worsens every single day. And even when you try your best, it still seems to never be enough. If you forget to call them back, you hope they understand. If you cancel plans, you hope they check up on you. It doesn't mean that you don't care, but maybe it just means life has gotten in the way again. Don't ever be upset with yourself for that. Don't ever forget to be gentle with your heart and with others' hearts. Remember to always be the low-maintenance friend everybody needs.

"WHAT DO I DO?"

Babe,

Life doesn't always need a plan.

Some of the most beautiful things in life come
from spontaneity.

LOVERS TO STRANGERS

He watched her drive off in her pickup truck
He looked at her so beautifully

Maybe love at first sight
Or maybe a long-time love

I could tell she was different
Just by the way he stared

You don't see stares like that very often
His eyes were glossed with a pretty sparkle

I hope she wasn't leaving forever
I hope she knows how much he loves her

AT LEAST WE'RE TOGETHER

What an uncanny feeling to be writing this book
Without tears falling onto my notebook

I'm just crying into your arms instead

HALF-FULL GLASS

Blue skies are always pretty
But what if they make me sad?

Your love has always been perfect
But what if it's perfect I can't stand?

WHERE'S THE FINISH LINE?

I've been running
For quite some time now

I've tried stopping
But I always fall

Sometimes a breath
Doesn't exist

And suffocation
Can never be stalled

Your touch bringing
Me back to earth

But your eyes yell,
"Rest now baby doll"

Dear Diary,

I'm finally 27! I'm going to be honest... didn't think I'd make it. Most of my life I was always so sure of what I wanted, but in the last 3 years I've never been so lost. Life didn't feel too purposeful, but I knew deep down I had purpose. BUT! I did it! I made it! I'm here! I'm so in love with being alive and most importantly I'm so in love with myself ♡

HIGH MAINTENANCE

Good morning texts

Remembering my favorite things

Walking me to my car

Hugs

Pinky promises

Goodnight texts

I was told I was high maintenance

he loves me

he loves me not

WISH US LUCK

I hope it's me.

Better yet,
I hope it's us.

YES, I DO

Remember when I said I don't see a stone?
I was so confused at the beginning of this all
Being with you for forever seemed frightening

"Mom, can you hold me in your arms tonight?"

Remember when I said I don't see a stone?
I love to say it, but I am so sure about you after all
Being with you for forever is a dream come true

"Baby, can you hold me in your arms tonight?"

"we'll take 2 please!
but they're both
for me."

SAVE YOURSELF

I've tried to rationalize my inconsistencies

Saying I love you tomorrow

Pushing you away today

It all makes sense in my head

Does it hurt less now?

I hope it does

I promise to hold you soon

Than push you away instead

If you run away

I won't be mad

But I'll never forgive you

A day that I will dread

WOW

I vow to forever love you, to carry your heart for as long
as I live, and if carrying yours falls heavy on my hands,
I promise to leave mine behind, to be soft with words
when my thoughts get harsh, and to listen when words
aren't needed, to continue to help you live life to its
fullest, to make sure every dream is achieved, and to
always be your home.

A SCARY THOUGHT

I fantasize of an English summer
Where taking a breath felt easy
Where you were all mine
Even the strangers called me greedy!

The sun would speak to us
And the flowers would shine

I'd lose you in the tall fields
I'd scream, "I LOVE YOU"
I'd scream, "WHERE ARE YOU?"
I'd scream, "I CAN'T LOSE YOU"

THANK YOU WILL NEVER BE ENOUGH

God only

      Knows

How much

      You

Saved me

      Baby

DON'T BE AFRAID TO LOVE YOUR FRIENDS

My love stories always seem to start off as friendships. Is it a blessing or a curse? I'm not really sure. It's a blessing because there's already trust established. Yet, it's a curse because you risk losing a friend forever. Oh well, but I cherish my love stories. I love the opportunity to love others passionately and unconditionally. I love knowing I'm capable of that. I truly believe there's nothing more beautiful than the ability to love. Despite some of my past love stories ending in turmoil and heartbreak, my current love story has left me speechless.

BALANCE

Sometimes it feels like my mind
Is the meeting point to heaven and hell

How can I scream at myself
When I know how to love myself so well

Dear Diary,

I got my period this morning and feel so horrible... does he even love me? I've been a little unbearable. I know I am because I can't even stand myself. I hope he doesn't leave me but I've left twice already. I'm so hypocritical. I wish I was pretty. I can't stand myself. It's 11 am and I'm going back to bed.

BUT I GAVE UP ON YOU

Do I call this love?
I do
Do you call this love?
I hope

I would say this is love
Because you never
Gave up on me

But I gave up on you

So you may have
A better word for
What this was

But I gave up on you

I told you I'd clean up my mess. even though I didn't want to.

YOUR TYPICAL LOVE STORY

From,

Strangers to friends

To best friends to enemies

To lovers to enemies

To,

Lovers again

HAPPY VALENTINE'S DAY

Last Valentine's Day was a little different
The two lovers were surrounded by strangers

They weren't sure how to act around one another
Because her heart was always choking her

They had a drink
Or maybe two
They wanted a kiss
That was overdue

"How are you?"
"I'm good and you?"
"I'm ok I guess"

They didn't really know what to say
But they both wanted each other to stay

As much as they wanted to leave
The two lovers stayed and grieved

EVERYDAY CONVERSATIONS

Speak beautifully about yourself now
We won't be beautiful for forever

Speak beautifully about yourself now
Go write yourself that letter

Speak beautifully about yourself now
We all grow old no pressure

forgive me I suck at drawing

I COULDN'T LOSE MY EGO

Looking through my tears
At a windshield view
I knew if I didn't call
You'd find someone new

Oh! I guess I was right
Just look at you two
My deep, darkest fears
Have finally come true

My deep, darkest fears
Have finally come true

PEACE TO ME

As much as I love us now
I think I might've loved us more back then

The unknown was always exhilarating . . .

If our love was enough
If we were going to fall apart

Something about it was comforting . . .

But now I'm so sure
We're really meant to be

I might not be comfortable
But I am finally at peace

SOME ADVICE FOR YOU

If you love someone, don't ever let them walk
away.

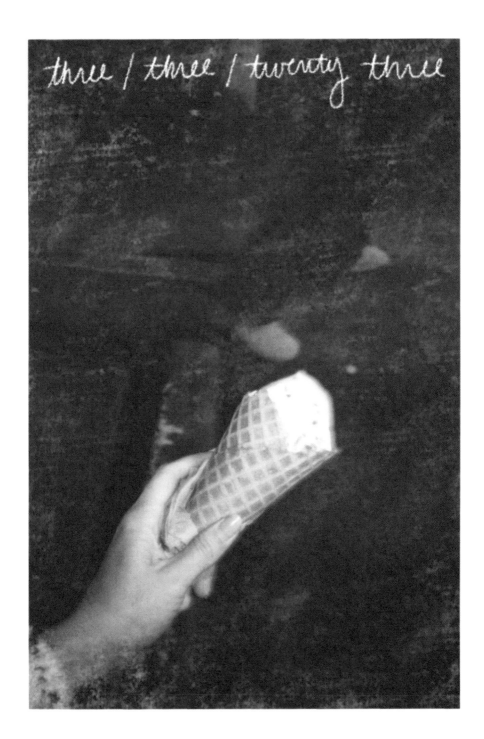

ANOTHER LIFETIME

Maybe in another life
    I loved myself enough
To not destroy the one
    Thing that fought for me

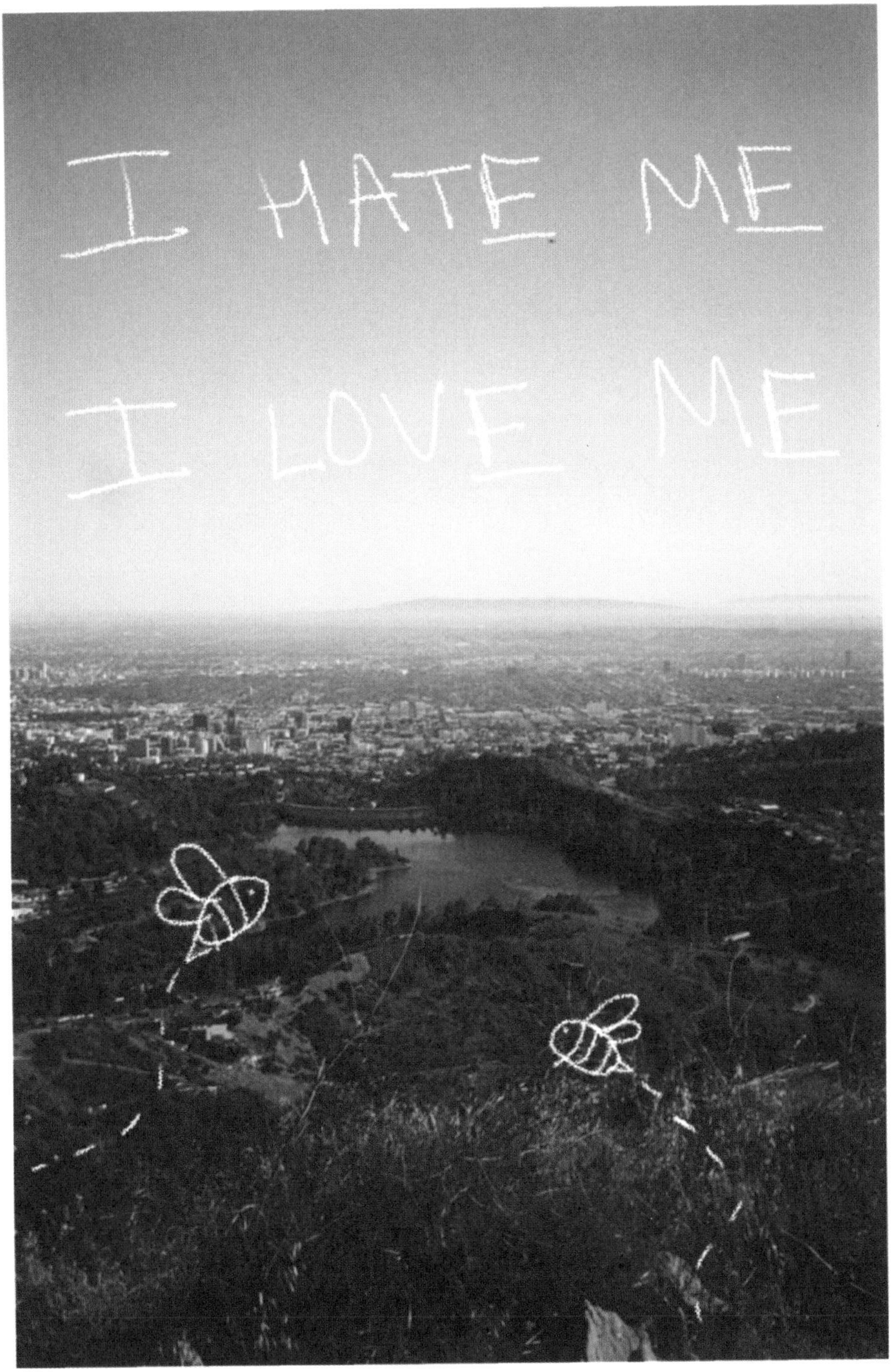
I HATE ME
I LOVE ME

THE GRASS IS ALWAYS GREENER ON THE OTHER SIDE

Thank you
for never
giving up
on me,
for the
90% I
didn't have.

To my baby!!

Hello from France & missing
you more and more every
single day

~~...~~

Ily France me

THE INVISIBLE STRING THEORY

I was once told that every single person on earth has a red string attached to their heart. On the other end of that string stands their soulmate. No matter the distance you go or the roadblocks you may encounter, the string stays. All you could ever want is for that string to reel you right into the person you are destined to be with. You can't see it now, but as you get older, the string shortens. As your heart heals, the string shortens. As you become nicer to yourself, the string shortens. I guess the string finally disappears when you can look at yourself in the mirror and say I love you.

POPSTAR 101

Don't meet your idols
They'll leave you sad

A RED LIGHT

Waiting at red lights is my favorite pastime
Just watching dozens of strangers drive by

Are they happy?
Are they in love?

Waiting at red lights is my favorite pastime
Just thinking about me, myself, and I

Am I happy?
Am I in love?

TULIPS

I wish I had stayed
A little longer

Just long enough to
Watch our flowers grow

Just to see what
They could've turned into

Just a little water
Nothing more

I might've left them
A little too early

They couldn't
Water themselves

I couldn't
Water myself

So they died
I died

The Little Things

And all you can really ask
is to find someone
you're happy to make
a cup of coffee for
every morning
for the rest of your life

I PUT THIS ON MY VISION BOARD AND IT CAME TRUE

And all you can really ask
is to find someone
you're happy to make
a cup of coffee
every morning for the
rest of your life

Writers

FIRST LOVE

If only I had you as a first love

What a beautiful first love that would've been

A love without heartache
A love without betrayal
A love without an end

I RAN FAR

At the end of the day
It's the person who never ran away

If the world was ending
Would you take me with you?

Things can be different
I know it's not the same

But I love you
I know I'm such a shame

CLARITY

My future's so clear and unclear.
I think I know what I want, but when I run for
it, I'm always stopped.
A roadblock.
A challenge.
Makes me second-guess the possibility that
any dream might not be real.
Just a brief thought, I guess.
But how could the visions be so vivid?
Every color, every shape, every tear.
Happy or sad.
I see it all.
I pray that God is near.
I pray He keeps it clear.

SCREAM IT

Love everyone in your life loudly
Make sure they can hear you from afar
Even if years have gone by
And no words have been spoken
If any ounce of you still loves them
Make sure that they know it

NO NEED TO SPEAK

Blink once if you hate me
Blink twice if you love me

I hope you don't hate me
I'm just learning to love me

GIRL BRAIN

*"Idk I think he just forgets or doesn't care
hahaha idk hard to say. It just flips my
emotions so fast. I'm like 'screw him honestly'
then he texts and I'm like 'aw ok he cares.
This could work' start fantasizing blah blah
blah.. then nothing and I'm like 'alright where
tf do we actually stand' lol. It's crazy making.
Mostly bc my brain is the way it is but ya"*
—Ellie Laufer

CAN YOU LEAVE NOW?

I MISS NINETEEN

One night, you're nineteen, driving through
Hollywood until sunrise, and your shift starts
at ten am. But it's ok; you feel free, nothing
really matters, and you're happy.

One night, you're twenty-six, at home in bed
by eight pm, and the sun hasn't even set yet.
But the thought of seeing anyone or feeling
anything terrifies you, and you're sad.

AT THE END OF THE DAY

I wish I hated you
In the nicest way

In a way that I can
Still love you every day

To hate you enough
To want to leave

To love you enough
To let you go

If only you had broken my heart

*Please don't forget about this book the next time
you're falling in love again.*